Guess What

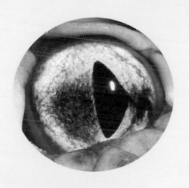

Published in the United States of America by
Cherry Lake Publishing
Ann Arbor, Michigan
www.cherrylakepublishing.com

Content Adviser: Susan Heinrichs Gray
Reading Adviser: Marla Conn, ReadAbility, Inc.
Book Design: Felicia Macheske

Photo Credits: © Eric Isselée/Shutterstock.com, cover, 18, backcover; © voylodyon/Shutterstock.com, 1, 4; Audrey Snider-Bell/
Shutterstock.com, 3, 11, 13; © mountainpix/Shutterstock.com, 7; © N. F. Photography/Shutterstock.com, 9; © Filip Fuxa/
Shutterstock.com, 14; © Fribus Mara/Shutterstock.com, 17, back cover; © fivespots/Shutterstock.com, 21; © Andrey_Kuzmin/
Shutterstock.com, back cover

Library of Congress Cataloging-in-Publication Data

Calhoun, Kelly, author.
 Slinky sliders / Kelly Calhoun.
 pages cm. – (Guess what)
 Summary: "Young children are natural problem solvers and always looking for answers, especially when it involves animals. Guess
What: Slinky Sliders: Rattlesnake provides young curious readers with striking visual clues and simply written hints. Using the photos
and text, readers rely on visual literacy skills, reading, and reasoning as they solve the animal mystery. Clearly written facts give
readers a deeper understanding of how the animal lives. Additional text features, including a glossary and an index, help students
locate information and learn new words"– Provided by publisher.
 Audience: Age 5-8.
 Audience: Grades K to 3.
 Includes index.
 ISBN 978-1-63362-631-7 (hardcover) — ISBN 978-1-63362-721-5 (pbk.) — ISBN 978-1-63362-811-3 (pdf) —
ISBN 978-1-63362-901-1 (ebook)
 1. Rattlesnakes—Juvenile literature. 2. Children's questions and answers. I. Title.

QL666.O69C35 2016
597.96'38—dc23

2015003099

Cherry Lake Publishing would like to acknowledge the work of The Partnership for 21st Century Skills.
Please visit *www.p21.org* for more information.

Printed in the United States of America
Corporate Graphics Inc.

Table of Contents

Pits near my eyes help me feel **heat.**

My tongue tastes the air.

My body is covered with scaly skin.

I have a rattle to warn you away.

Rattle Rattle

I have sharp fangs.

Watch out!

I **coil** my **body** **to protect myself.**

I shed my skin so I can grow.

I have a long body and no legs.

Do you know what I am?

I'm a Rattlesnake!

About Snakes

1. A snake can flick out its tongue to "taste" the air when it's hunting.

2. Snakes eat mice, small birds, and lizards.

3. All snakes shed their skin once in a while, to allow them to keep growing.

4. Grown-up rattlesnakes eat about every two weeks.

5. Most snakes are afraid of humans.

Glossary

coil (coyl) to wind into loops or rings

fangs (fangz) an animal's long, pointed teeth

pits (pitz) holes from which something is being dug out

rattle (RAT-uhl) to make a series of short, sharp noises

scaly (SKALE-ee) covered in thin, flat, overlapping pieces of hard skin

shed (shed) to cast off or get rid of

Index